promised instruments

SERIES EDITORS

John Alba Cutler
Reginald Gibbons
Susannah Young-ah Gottlieb
Ed Roberson

promised instruments

poems

Kristiana Rae Colón

NORTHWESTERN UNIVERSITY PRESS

EVANSTON, ILLINOIS

Northwestern University Press
www.nupress.northwestern.edu

Northwestern University Poetry and Poetics Colloquium
www.poetry.northwestern.edu

Printed in the United States of America

10 9 8 7 6 5 4 3 2

Library of Congress Cataloging-in-Publication Data
Colón, Kristiana Rae.
    Promised instruments : poems / Kristiana Rae Colón.
        p. cm.—(Drinking gourd chapbook series)
    ISBN 978-0-8101-2891-0 (pbk. : alk. paper)
    I. Title. II. Series: Drinking gourd chapbook series.
PS3603.O464P76 2013
811.6—dc23

                                                    2012027983

♾ The paper used in this publication meets the minimum requirements
    of the American National Standard for Information Sciences—
Permanence of Paper for Printed Library Materials, ANSI Z39.48-1992.

Contents

Acknowledgments

I would like to thank Roger Reeves, Roger Bonair-Agard, Phillip Williams, and Tara Betts. Without their guidance, thoughtful critique, and loving encouragement, these poems could not exist. "ex libris" was first published in *Our Stories* and later in Dzanc Books' *Best of the Web 2010*. "intra" and "a daughter" were first published in *Diverse Voices Quarterly*. "post" and "severance" were first published in *Organs of Vision and Speech,* by which it was nominated for a Pushcart Prize. "first service" first appeared in *Hinchas de Poesía*. "safe word" and "stranger fruit" were first published by the *African American Review*. "ash" and "the true vine" were first published by the *Logan Square Literary Review*. "instructions for giving" and "the pilgrimage of mouths" were first published by *PANK*. I thank the editors and readers of all of these publications for their support and appreciation of my work.

Foreword

Ed Roberson

Kristiana Rae Colón's *promised instruments,* a poetic sequence of dramatic monologues, has won The Drinking Gourd Prize from Northwestern University Press for a first chapbook. Colón, besides being the prize winning poet, is also a performance artist and ensemble member of Chicago's Teatro Luna.

One of the most fascinating challenges in both writing and reading dramatic monologue is the thread of the left unsaid. One of the strands in that thread is the nature of the character speaking; another is the reader's interest as the writer develops in that character; a third and most exciting is watching the writer appear and disappear in and out of each position at just the right time, escaping with just the right object to keep open the question: what's going on here? Colón's skilled contemporary use of the serial technique is one way she keeps the poem moving.

But one of her skills has an even stronger hold on my attention: the impact she builds within a single object. This is not the thriller of W. C. Williams, the ax murderer, but the material things in her work do get a little edgy, and often to that end of a self-deprecating humor. Colón's diction may be clearly self-aware plain speak, but her rhetoric twists and turns to reveal a deeply intelligent emotional life. An old fiction's telltale cigarette is the source of a quiet, ironic chuckle here. The deeply felt jealousy of a wife suddenly appearing to cut up the papaya the "other-woman" had intended for her lover is all shocking contrasts of color, texture of skin and knife, those little black buckshot seeds and, of course, that bloody sweet juice. Colón has a very gutsy grip on her art, not only in ways to weight her images, but in ways to make a dialogue activate an idea.

the pilgrimage of mouths

My throat is a winding staircase
of stone, where words pace up
to my teeth's narrow apertures
and dare jump. Other nights

I choke on their clumsy catapult down
into the roil of my belly, a cauldron stoked
by slow sipping a twelve-year Barbadian

rum. I approach the decade with eyes
focused ahead, squinting to discern the unfamiliar

shape growing edges against the dark
like an animal slowing in the center of the road:
a woman wearing green mascara and rabbit

fur, resisting nothing, delivering two naked bodies
into the other's mouth, remember my mouth

was full of bullets I let dribble to my living
room hardwood one at a time, blackbirds falling
from the aviary of my jaws. Some nights
my throat is a rifle's cold catheter holding

breath, a sacral growl threatening to unsteady
the trigger, but not on this first morning.
In the year of car keys left dangling in the ignition
of my locked Dodge, a future lover with a wooden wedge
and a hammer, my throat is a blade's narrow sheath,

a panopticon caging the columnar waver of a question
or a poem or an apology. Before I can earn forgiveness

I must first fumble the rum glass too near
his piano, and then my throat becomes a lighthouse

and every lover I'll have this year is churning oars
toward the intermittent fingers of light I send
curling into the black grain of months

yet to learn the density of sound. My ribs
are a parapet for the pilgrimage of mouths
whose poems are not metaphors for kisses; no longer
a pharaoh's third bride wafting through his sarcophagus
apartment, kicking clay pots of honey, crushing jade locusts
against the final hieroglyphs, intent on wailing the corpse
awake, this year my throat is a pillar of its own, a monument naked
of epitaphs or erasures, helix of sex
and sound, mouth rounding to name
what time has left unnamed.

intra

The doctor's erected a pyramid
inside my uterus, a crucifix

I sport a tangle of copper
atop my cervix, tiny bracelets

wound around the stoic
sentry stationed in my womb

He is a soldier, a boned
scarecrow. My children kneel

for his sword; he unravels helixes,
splinters the blueprints for brows,

hazel, height, lashes, coarse,
freckles, arithmetic, he doesn't blink.

Just strangles sleeping embryos. Dices
nucleotides to ribbons, confetti decorating

the fallopian halls where generations would hang
and sleep and tussle through fluid, daughters

never to grow hair enough for plaits,
or lungs, or flesh enough for tumors,

sons never to be fleshed at all
The doctor's propped a rifle

against the red wall, bullets
shatter meiotic membranes, painters and pianists

die in the crossfire. How many presidents
have curdled in my menses since?

How many rapists and athletes
and architects? How many

astronomers have averted abortion,
their births so strictly controlled

a daughter

I think I smothered your child
in my quiet churn, muzzled her
tiny African mandible in the mucous
of my undone motherhood, braided

black cables of her hair into bone
marrow, burned her fingernails to crust,
crushed the song of ashen atoms twisting
in the thimble of her throat. I wanted you

to save her, to hear her
when you mined me. I was only silence
for you to plumb, air too thin
to womb for your songs. When you stab

a brittle matchbox with a staff
of dynamite, something is sure to burn.

in winter

When the heater sparked the carpet we dreamed
of the east, Egypt, sphinxes, hippopotami thrashing
in courtyard fountains, palace marble and sand

In his I was Jasmine naked
and we moaned the moon full

In mine we kayaked the Nile
but got lost in tangled mangroves

The pain dissolved in dust of loving
slumber, hands knotted at knuckles we held
through flames; the black mattress framed our bones

melted to ampersand

Why the Woman Undecided Leaving,
or I Became a Ghost at Luis Muñoz Marín

When your woman sits across your kitchen island smiling
at the glint of your curved blade halving the horn
of coral papaya I bought to thank you for our Sunday
lovemaking, I urge my ghost to keep quiet in the corners,
to still its flitting reflection in the island's flat granite, to knot

herself into the pink light summer sun slicks across your kitchen
hardwood. I don't want it to disturb the chaste love, the woman's
earnest fingers searching your palms, to clutter the air with silly plucking
of the guitar strings muscling your spine.
I'd hoped to cut the papaya myself,

to start with neat cubes giving way to hacked slabs
as anticipation swelled. But just as well that you gut
its black seeds for her, spoon its sticky middle
into the blender, add crushed ice and modest dregs
of our favorite black rum, hold the black button

for liquefy, balance its fury under your thumb arching
into your palm, search her eyes for some shadow that she knows
I am here, while the fruit reconstitutes itself in her honor.

When she dreams, she is in Old San Juan,
the hard leather of her sandals cracking
to grip the colonial cobblestone. Another woman's husband
panics at her beauty in the dim street and she pulls you
by your thumb into the doorway of a restaurant
she'll never know I recommended.

The bartender will float rose petals in a cocktail that doesn't dull
the sense that my laugh quakes in the clatter of her fork to the stone
floor. When she sleeps, her spine is an ampersand
nestling into your chest, you trace the curves of her face

and forget efforts to silence my shadow hanging
in your closet like a bat.

She is dreaming El Morro blots the ocean moon,
that its dungeons muffle manacled ghosts
of slaves singing into the angry tide. There's an open market
in Plaza de Colón today, where daughters of slaves sell
bracelets carved of kola nut or coral, and she loses your face
in the crowd. Hundreds of husbands are shoving trinkets at her,
shouting their song that *parcha helado* is only two dollars,
a freshly hacked coconut only one. But she doesn't want their fruit,
only for your thumb to appear in her palm, you lilting
her panic aside to say "I'm here. I'm here."

When I return on Tuesday to find the papaya gone,
I ask my ghost to gather our bracelets from your bathroom
sink, pack away the wide-toothed comb clutching clumps of our curls
in your shower, reconstitute the flecks of skin forming our scent
in your knotted bedsheets. But your woman has already collected them
    all, the muffled shriek of my shadow desperate to escape
the plaza of her dark dreams.

When she lays them out on the flat granite of the kitchen island,
like a set of knives for you to consider, they are songless, inert.
You wonder where I am that I'm not here.

severance

From the outset the fingers were cursed. They blackened
and liquefied at the nail beds, green tendrils
of fungus snaked over knuckles, carpals
crushed to mush and the elbow
was next. I just kept filling the sink
with iodine. I told the grocer

my three-year-old had jabbed pencil lead
through the right palm, and the fist was gauze
wrapped for eight days excepting the nightly baptism, white
porcelain slopped full of blood brown iodine
sloshing up to the feet of the toothbrushes.
I tried peroxide mornings.

The crusting hole fizzed and crackled like Christmas
ornaments crushed to snow in my palm. I told the daycare

it was Sunday dinner, a knife
slipped off the round of an onion and clipped
the web of skin stretched between fingers. The mothers
gave me remedies scribbled on grainy gray pads
of coloring paper and dragged away their mittened brats
to the minivans. I cancelled and cancelled and cancelled

appointments at the clinic. That's when the mitt began
to black. I told my mother I'd been typing long hours;

I'd never told her I'd been fired in July.
My husband never asked.

It is a good hand, a held hand, a hand
woven with lovers' in fireworks grass,
a hand that bends around its left to lift
the wedding band away during dishes.

It is a hand that cradles cakes of soap
in the bath and holds a swath of nieces'
hair for the braiding, a hand whose florid
scrawl ended letters, whose aged weight
answered insults with smacks.

The end of it chokes up the elbow
toward the shoulder. I ache against

my sling. There is an axe
in the tool shed he used
for the swingset, hanging
on a nail I can't reach.

first service

Stanley Rivers took me
to play tennis on Saturdays. We served
over the stretch of nets, ulna
bending under to flick
wrist through racket.
My mother let Stanley
Rivers teach me to play
tennis. Endless after-
noon spill on sofa after,
lemonade and sand-
wiches. I watch
movies with girls
who are daughters
of girlfriends with sofas
and board games. Cigarette smoke
net over island of kitchenette.
Stanley Rivers buckled
me into his Nissan. He promised
my mother I would get home
safe. Stanley Rivers's hand
handled the handle
of the racket hardly. White stripe
striked over the stitch
of net slicing the brown
belly of the court. I deadnet
and score sometimes but he
beats me every time.

ash

On the corner of Spaulding and Crystal, a black girl asked to use my
cell phone. Tears froze on her sickle lashes and the blink of the blue light
camera danced in the tiny ice like a strobe. Streaks of salt striped her dark
cheek where earlier streams had dried. I did not have gloves and she did
not either and we shivered on the corner under the medicinal glow of
street lamps. A rim of faux fur flopped against her shoulders as the over-
sized hood of her metallic black puff coat slipped off her hatless head.
Her fingers searched the keys. They were stiff from cold. I tapped against
the concrete and puffed out my lips. I blew streams of breath into the
sunless eager dusk. She dialed and dialed. Frayed skin from her chapped
lips clumped and crusted in the corners of her mouth. He would not
answer. She gurgled that she needed a ride and dialed one last number.
The answerer gave her someone else to call and she dipped her chin to her
collar to hold the phone as she scratched a phone number into the dry
black skin of her hand with her fingernail. The number shone ash white
above her knuckles. She thanked me for the phone and pulled the hood
back over her face. I searched the winter air for something to do, but there
was just nothing.

a spell

I once placed a marble in your palm:
by morning it was a knot of thread

Once rubbed your heels with olive
oil: by sunset your feet grew scales

There were bougainvilleas blooming in a howl
that rounded out my throat when we made love:

by weekend your brothers painted whore
on my windows; every miracle I conjured

in your name was a disemboweled hog
before I could say love; every magic

turned brackish before I learned
to lie; once my back arched to offer you passage:

you tried to pave my thigh with pitch
The last talisman a woman sows

under a lover's pillow is fate, rotting
like the roots of fallen teeth; every song

I warbled moonside was in the key of fallen teeth
Once I singed suras on the femur of a steed:

every tercet turns ash when you sing

safe word

::: the poet meets the band

I am the lonely vixen haunting jazz
clubs, carving moons into the soft wood
of the bar with nervous fingernails. Tension

is solvent and whatever cocktail's on special
will soften the day's angst splinting
lower vertebrae. Imperceptible sway

balanced on black barstools, scribbling in the net
of light cast by shallow candles, and after
only a few cherrybottomed glasses, I am

ready to stop pretending I'm not pliant. There's no danger
in folding my secrets into bar napkins, into the flapping magic
music of saxophones, no danger in the dark tower of sound

winding up from the front man's mouth. No one
has to know there's more than unwritten verses
aching beneath my dress, snaking through my palms

to be heard. There's no danger in applause,
in mumbling invitations drowned
out by the heaving impetus of drums.

morning music

::: pantoum for the drummer

His black hands thrust a crash against cymbals
Skin stretched tight for his pounds
Bitten tongues burn pink through irregular rhythms
Schism of silence between sound and applause

Skin stretched tight for his pounds
Knuckles find neck a bundle of drumsticks
Schism of silence between sound and applause
No hide can hide where his song sounded raw

Knuckles find neck a bundle of drumsticks
Stick fingers through ribs like a gun
No hide can hide where his song sounded raw
Dare her screams to sound louder than plick-ums and trill

Stick fingers through ribs like a gun
Carve throne from the bones of her hips
Dare her screams to sound louder than plick-ums and trill
Resistance is hissed but drowns in the snare

Carve throne from the bones of her hips
Snare ankles and wrists in his fists
Resistance is hissed but drowns in the snare
and pupils that blare while lips remain stitched

Snare ankles and wrists in his fists
then flip her to dig through resonant rim
and pupils that blare while lips remain stitched
till breath is a hi-hat that glitters his rifts

Then flip her too, dig through resonant rim
Bitten tongues, burn pink through irregular rhythms
till breath is a hi-hat that glitters his rifts
His black hands thrust a crash against cymbals

band practice

::: the drummer's handmade gift

The man who has mastered nailing
her knees open with his own also makes bracelets
of copper and amber for a lover that is not her.

He winds soft wires around soft wood
and stones, winces when a sharp edge taps blood
from his nail bed; he taps his foot when the lover

inhales to begin a song, in the yawn of air
before the first splash of his drum. His drum
crushed the air before the skin, and his lover

peeled open air with her voice. Her voice
was never the voice of knees nailed open
with knees, but that woman does not sing.

Her voice will not climb the wire of her
throat. Not even when he drums her.
He molds his lover a gift of wire

and wood and stone, a gift she wears with her song
when it's rising through wrists she drums
over piano keys. Which is to say the singer

is accompanied by an excellent percussionist,
a man who holds open doors, who masters copper.
The singer will kiss his nail bed, kiss the callus

on the drumstick of his thumb. Her voice
is amber. Her wooden knees
when she receives his gift are closed.

black is the color

::: the singer doubts her story

In his basement I cover Nina,
lean into the smooth clicking teeth
of my keyboard. He beams behind his kit, tapping
gentle time, brushing cymbal grooves with the seed

shaped tip of his left stick. He's loved me desperately,
an infant lapping at a mother's infrequent tit.
His skin is too dark for bruises. One winter
afternoon, I mounted him in the cheap

heat of his bedroom, raking my nails across the black
seeds of his nipples, watching his face contort
in wild grief, expecting to smell her sex
in the eyes of his denim. I drummed my hips
into his. Instead I smelled the oil she fingers
through her hair and I know it's her

because she likes our music; she pulls
tiny wrinkled legal pads from leather purses
and scribbles under the apple glow of cocktail
glasses while we play. She thanks me

for my voice after each set. So the smell of her hair
has gone home with me too. The bartender
at the spot we play used to like our music.
She sent over glasses twinkling with cold

Stoli after each set. But once, after a week of stoic cold,
she came with a ring of bruises around
her throat like a laurel. She won't look at me.
When I sing, she slinks to the bathroom.

chance encounters

::: the poet hides in the parking lot

It could happen any day. Mid afternoon in the produce,
they are chuckling through the spray over bell peppers,
she checks the firmness of a black plum. She's the type that sings
everywhere. Scats into the eggplant. I often lose my balance
in the shower, lift each breast to scrub underneath, scraping
parabolas of lather till my ribs glow pink. Or at a stoplight.

He's drumming the dashboard and she's singing
over the steering wheel. We're circling the same parking lot.
I see the plates of their jasper lacquered Jeep and drive away
without getting the eggs. I pray. I find a new grocery. I slip
in the tub. She doesn't know all the beats he plays. I want
to tell her. She sings over produce and laughs

when he bites her fingers. Her nail cracks the skin
of a firm black plum. It's definitely their license plate, so I pass
a row of parking spaces. He asked if he could come
to my birthday. I didn't say.
I was so wet, I wasn't even
sure I'd be able to scream.

geometry lesson

::: the drummer forces the poet

I play little games to distract, count
how many stabs I can hold
my breath, count spiders, close
my left eye so he vanishes, close
my knee twenty degrees, calculate
the angle necessary to eject him,
calculate the calories consumed
the day before, how many more cookies
I might have eaten had I known
how my belly'd be flayed by zippers
whose teeth jabber up and down, by denim
whose buttons and open eyes mock
my futile twisting. Memory
is treason. I chide myself
to stay alert, collect the timbre
of his smiling edicts, the sequence
of limbs, recite them in meter like verses
I must commit. I am counting again.
Windshields of passing cars, distant ambulance wails,
days till Christmas. Backwards
pillow
        silence
throat
        fingers
giggle
        zipper jabber
knee angle
        failed ejection
failed rejection
        failed comfort storytelling.
Remember?

Remember how his mother left?
How she had just returned
to scoop a grown son in her breast?
What did I say? What did I say
that made his eyes die?
I can't remember. I can't remember.

promised instruments

::: the poet doubts her story

I did invite him
over, flutter ice scythe lashes
against the steel of January night.
I did indulge language
arching across the moat of want
for common tongues, the sun surely played
in my morning hair, surely spelled consent
in flecks of light twisted on my lazy bathroom sink
dye job. He was reckless smile, limbs
too electric to not beat something

and there were no drums in my bedroom.
Perhaps I had promised an instrument.

Somewhere in the haze of midnight metaphysics
we exchanged a vow to become the medium

and some might say I got the better end of the bargain.
Just one morning posing as a glittering kit, hollow
enough to resound, a click clack clattering bones rhythm,
frantic jazz breathing in the batting of a cheap pillow
used to dampen the acoustics of screams
that never came. Bruises that would disappear
like quarter notes blown into the air.

And in return, he offered to flatten his flesh forever—
empty measures for all my selfish ink.

stranger fruit

::: the poet bargains with the band

There are no apologies in drums.
The square-toothed tenor goes on
lying through his song, the bass
chisels a little wound on the hip
of stage air, and yes there is a trumpet
whose open mouth is frozen in brass
screams. The inexorable percussion
is not sorry for the danger they play.

The door behind the stage opens to the alley.
A woman there would have screamed.
The walls of this joint pucker
like busted cheeks. The tick tick of drums
offers no apology, no recompense for torn hose, for muffling
the scream she might have hatched
if it weren't all so pointless. She hums along
with the blood of the trumpet instead.

The percussion isn't sorry, even when its rattle
quakes through alley bruises. The band just covers
summertime over and over, thrusting into medallions
of flesh peering through torn hose, dark melodies
clotting on the razor of her smile.

If she happens to addle the padlock rusting
against gurgles gagged in dumpster shadows, if
she trips on to the stage to ask the band for help,
losing her balance in the thicket of cymbals, if.

Nothing. She'll just twist
silently in branches of sound,
quizzical bruised fruit no one
dare speak.

post

some times your scent is gasoline
pickling a soldier's entrails. your touch, a phantom
dagger itching at my trachea, an empty swing
clanking on the spine of april snow. my fingers

twitch on the holster of my sidearm; i dream death
and kick the sheets that hold us sleeping. our past battles left scars.
some times your lips are charred flesh smoking through vines, some
times the graves are clawed open

by a drifting dandelion seed or saxophone
solos in the subway. i never know
what will do it. forgiveness is only forever

as my next night terror. some times
the guns chime against the flank of dawn. if i pop
my knuckle on the trigger, i'm only aiming at your ghost. some
times the screams scraping

me awake are tangled on my canines.
no wonder i am begging to be choked.

oil

Estherwood is two hours west
of Killona, so don't ask me
how a carload of spooks ended
up rattling in to Shelby's Fuel
and Service after closing time
while me, Mitch, and Pierre
squeezed beer out of Pabst cans
after our brothers kicked Crowley ass
on the little league field.

Don't get the wrong idea.
I only say spooks to give
the general feel of the thing;
I was just thinking of putting them back
on the highway and drinking another beer
but Pierre was awfully bored. Spooks
is just the kind of thing a hick like him
would say. Mitch and me drive to Baton Rouge
every July the fourth just to see the pretty black girls

and there was one pretty black girl in the back
of the Buick sputtering up to a gas pump
but Shelby's closes at seven.

And Mitch doesn't even like to kill
dragonflies when they smack the glass
of his patio door and lay squirming on the hot
wood porch. If we're out there drinking
lemonade Pierre'll probably stomp them,
but Mitch likes to set them in the grass
So don't get the wrong idea.

I was there but it wasn't my fault; bad things
happen all the time every second all over
the world and there's no one to blame.
Estherwood's full of civil folk,
folk who wouldn't lift a finger to a dragon
fly.

the true vine

A bottom tooth's been chipped
all the years he knew to love me,
red cilia of tongue catching in the sharp
groove like threads of my winter coat snagged
on a jagged chain fence. And who's the girl
whose mouth didn't work around the sugary ache,
sucking and prodding infinitesimal loss
of a bone that doesn't mend when broken?
And isn't the legend of Babel a crock?
A god so little and vain that towers can reach
her, that hearts must tangle *treason* and *treasure*
to excise our memory of being living dirt
rolled wet between her plump thumbs.
We mustn't flatter ourselves.

We spent that first Thanksgiving naked
in play of nomenclature, defining what cracks
and what can be splinted. The tiny chasm
in my tooth raking blood out of kisses
and shoulders; I sang *Gloomy Sunday*
and *Stabat Mater* till the words turned chalk
in my jaws. Somewhere in time humans are sweating
toward heaven, to speak something of the self to a god
that rotates primly in the mirror of her sky. Words and bones
and bricks are all the same mess, all the same dream
of a firmament we can harden by giving it name.

I want to introduce him to the comma
of tooth that disappeared somewhere, into bowels
or apples or a stale baguette, into the grooves
of a chewed pen that soon ran dry of ink.
I want to introduce him to a god
unafraid of names lisping up through clouds,
shouted from minarets of our most audacious towers,
whistling through the canyons in our mouths.

instructions for giving

I wrapped the gifts in one man's
living room and stacked them
into my Maxima to drive to another's.
One was impressed with the care given
to each precise crease, the attention
to hiding lines of tape, the symmetry
of identical snowflakes falling over
the boxes' edges, the single blade
of sewing scissors scraping along
the ridged underside of the wisps
of silver ribbon, its wild helix erupting
from my sharp knots. The other was silent

and angry when I left his bed Christmas morning
to pull on jeans without sex. One man would later slap

my cheek as I perched in my panties on the edge
of his tub sobbing with scissors poised on the ribbon
of my veins, tired of being an unopened present

for the other man. Distinctions are peripheral.
First, you place the gift on the blank swath
of paper, intuit equidistance and cut, let the blade
glide like a tear from one edge to the other, like a lover
crossing the city in a Maxima doomed to crash, fold both
sides to the center crisply, obscuring adhesive
as though the wrap will stick by magic. The sides
are tricky, a labyrinth of triangles. Precision is paramount.

Once the gift is secure in its sheath of shimmer and hope
for some glimmer of gratitude, then comes the joy
of ribbons, royal purple and crimson crisscrossed
and absolute, with no indication of where each thread

begins. They culminate in a celebration of ringlets
cascading. This is the type of giving. The bliss
of a lover ripping through knots to receive me, and me
expecting nothing in return.

.

volcán irazú

I woke trembling on the slate gray carpet
of a Floridian airport outside my gate to San José
and the flight monitors flashed a red CANCELLED
beside every line to Port-au-Prince. The earth
had swallowed it, gargled the city's concrete and rebars,
dust and aluminum and legs severed at the knee churning
in her tectonic jaws, while me and my lover slept.

CNN warbled death tolls through our concourse
as we gathered carry-ons and prepared to present boarding
passes. The Costa Rican car rental would freeze one thousand
dollars in my checking account and we would drink Imperial
in the hammocks strung across the veranda of our bed and breakfast.
Five days in Samara with no television, we marooned ourselves
from quake coverage, sunburned and ziplined and spelunked.
We kept no count of survivors, inured to apocalypse featuring black
tears and torn flesh; we kayaked, and snorkeled, but the tide
was too high to reach the coral. On our final day

we drove to the volcano. Wound our way up mountains, passed
the ragged shanties and water pumps, the wild goats bleating dumbly
beside narrow, sinuous roads we dared. The air thinned
and we dizzied in raw sun. When we finally reached Irazú's
ashen crest, it was all black rock, shimmering secret deaths,
the ancient goats the lava surely drowned, the farmers' bones
rung for oil under the weight of a thousand mountains, the feathers
that adorned the hair of shepherds' eldest daughters, feathers of juncos
choked in the soot earth once spat through her savage stone teat,
all hidden under smooth igneous basalt, glinting like parking lot asphalt

in white sun. I stumbled breathing clouds
and my thumbs began to plump
so we snapped a few stagnant
shots, tried to capture the majesty

of primordial black magma,
and retreated to the rental, blasting
a/c back to the airport. I gasped

all the air I could; we were fossils, and boarding back
to where edges of the earth were crumbling
faster than our feet could find ground.

instructions for the next heartbreak

It's okay. It's okay to staple your curtains over the sun,
to let your bones grow long and drag out
of their sockets like extension cords teasing
from the hiss of their nest beneath the desk
he carried up and down three flights of apartment
stairs. It's okay to remember how many pounds
you weigh without lungs full of another's breath,
how night becomes a toothless cackle when stars
have been plucked away like bits of shell from the raw
egg slop the sky keeps trying to pass off as sky,
it's okay to roam the three rooms of your apartment
as though he might be hiding in any one of them,
smiling, waiting, like a parent in a cartoon costume
to surprise a birthday child, to calm your shaking,
say it was all just a joke, to say it was all just a test
to see how high the flames the flint of your clumsy ribs
could raise once you stopped eating. It's okay to dig
holes in the beams of your back porch and plant
shards of the bowl you battered against the wall
to blot out your screams, to water this strange garden
with webs of blood that balloon from your throat
like bubble gum each time you try to pronounce
his name. It's okay to rake your ankles across
the asphalt of Lake Shore Drive and perch naked
on the median like a steel-beaked gull and squawk
at the traffic that you'll let no one help you down
but him, that you know he'll come, that he'll skid
to the shoulder any minute now and lace his limbs around
you, pitch a sweater over your purpling breasts, blow
the hypothermia out of your fingernails, kiss
apologies into your elbows. It's okay to hail
a cab when he doesn't, to let the scabs of your lips
glisten like two mating beetles under the gloss
you apply in the driver's rearview, to dare

the driver to chase you into your courtyard
when you slam the cab door without paying
your fare. It's okay to keep revising your obituary,
adding that you were the one who shook three days
of snow from the thunder thatching black clouds,
scratching out survived by loving husband and two
beautiful daughters, scratching out the list of names
he made in your diary, scratching out the pearls
of memory that keep pimpling the places he last
kissed, blistering the path his hands
last traveled in the valley of your back.
It's okay to be kissed again, to finally
take the blender out of the box, to find
a morning when your floorboards are warm
enough to fill it with cinnamon and frozen
peaches. It's okay to dismantle the chandelier
of rum bottles, the windchime of kitchen knives
whose winter piccolo whistled your night terrors
alive. It's okay to peel yourself out of yourself
& shuck away the shell. It's okay to swell into a god
when you find yourself still breathing
& with all ten of your digits accounted for, to assure
the audience a tongue will grow back when you promise
the magic trick of gutting yours from the cobwebbed coffin
of your jaws onstage, you've done this before
and you know it will be okay. You will love
and bleed and love and bleed and love
until you stop believing love requires quartered
limbs or quarts of blood or coins for the ferry.
It's okay to tell the ferryman to go on without you,
you've misplaced the quarter for the toll and anyway
it's okay that you're here now, it's okay to be

here now. You're here now.

You're here.

Kristiana Rae Colón is a poet, playwright, actor, and educator living in Chicago. She has been featured on the HBO television series *Def Poetry Jam* and on WBEZ's Chicago Public Media. Her work has been nominated for a Pushcart Prize honoring the best writing published in small presses, and it has been anthologized in *Not a Muse* (2009), *Best of the Web 2010,* and the upcoming collection *Chorus: A Literary (Re)Mixtape,* an anthology of poetry by young people edited by Saul Williams and Dufflyn Lammers.